COMING
&
GOING

by Julian Stan

Cover & Interior Design: Julian Stan

Front cover photo: Monika Kozub via Unsplash photo app

Back cover photo: Valentin Beauvais via Unsplash photo app

ISBN: 9798352210734

Julian Stan
London, United Kingdom

For merch, books, and original functional NFTs visit
www.arkdian.com.
Insta: @arkdian

www.linkedin.com/in/julianstan

www.portocal.app
Twitter: @arkdianOfficial
Spotify: @arkdian
For Life Coaching Packages contact Julian directly via the channels above.

ABOUT THE AUTHOR

Julian Stan is a British/Dacian (Romanian) author, influencer and entrepreneur living in London. He grew up and studied in the beautiful seashore city of Constanta, close to the most famous resort on the Black Sea, Mamaia, also called the "Miami of Europe". He owns a Bachelor's degree in Economics from Ovidius University - Constanta, and a post-grad in Border Force Tactics, Travel Documents, and International Law.

Before deciding to permanently move abroad, he served as a Border Force/Coast Guard officer for almost a decade. In the UK he worked for three years in biotechnology as a laboratory technician in the large scale fractionation of the human blood plasma, with Bio Products Laboratory. He decided to become self-employed in 2020, in order to expand his businesses and live a beautiful life.

He is also the author of the one-of-a-kind partially autobiographical novel **This is my Electronica**, *about his love for electronic music, DJ-ing, and Ibiza. This work is unique in his native country.*

In 2021 he published his second non-fiction novel, **Kiss the Girl Save the World Kill the Baddie**, *a unique collection of revelating personal experiences.*

Contents

Foreword

These poems are some of the best from this promising experimental writer. They evoke the natural spirit of man, and when around a woman, in this case his woman and her powerful character. With a complete literary emotion that gives you thrills and a perfectly balanced taste for lust, he gives the world his anticipation of the most common, soft, and complex desires. Leaving no room for error in judgment, the verse takes shape more inside of you than it does on paper. At the end, you find yourself with the seed of craving for carnal pleasure planted directly into your soul. Giving his natural and unique style, he is among the few writers that can make you want to read more about the magical bond between man and woman, in an ideally sexual context. His passion shows on every turn and for the future, this kind of writing can drive us right into the realms of subliminal exploration and understanding of woman and the Universe. Make contact with high class philosophy inside the lyrics, and enjoy the start of this beautiful and sensitive journey, of "Coming & Going".

mile alive

Grained tarmac,

I feel you sharp and rough

through my sport shoes with thin sole.

Limply I fall resoundingly,

while a pothole interrupts my rhythm.

Although I instinctively avoid making the wrong steps,

a whole life turns us into cowards.

I rise lively,

pharisee,

not knowing if I'm doing good.

I stare at the road I need to go,

and see perfection in all.

I could not anticipate

the obstacle that kneeled me down,

although, I underestimated nothing.

As I make the first step

I decide to live.

The foot on which I fell

makes me aware to lift it

higher,

and when pain travels the distance with speed,

I force myself to continue.

The asphalt elongates impeccably

toward the horizon.

I see all a cliché, but enigma attracts me

to know.

I'm alone on this road,

and see people on the field.

I don't understand why they're shouting at me
crazy.

While alone on my road

something is shoving me,

but I can't see a thing

to fight with.

I oppose with immense fear,

but I can tame it when I notice

that it tries

to take me off track,

while the people are getting closer.

They're making me desperate signs

to give up

my effort from instinct,

to get off the impossible road,

and follow them

to disgrace.

Then I slip sideways

with my good leg.

I'm human as them

but infinite,

and see that a step if I make

they fall way behind.

Because they cannot be

on the same road with me,

in my soul,

I walk forward.

I catch up with many others

in my run,

and their advice to give up

turns into hands.

Crazy people grab me

by my dirty clothes,

of dust,

I take cover.

I protect my wounds

against the crazy attack.

I suddenly have no more power

to fight.

From avoidance I find myself in need

to startle, to lose them,

and my wounds number

is ever a constant.

With a single step I break

from the turmoil.

More wrinkled are they,

ten paces behind me,

and when I strengthen,

forgetting about my wounded foot,

I hit

...

a stone rock

appeared on the tarmac

from nowhere.

It makes me scream in pain

cause we struck each other.

Needing to lean

onto my injured leg,

I wonder

about the road I have chosen.

Pain is now divine.

It carries me like a drug

with every step.

I refuse to complain,

to think of regret,

to look back,

and ahead I see just

fulfilment.

The tarmac gets hotter underneath,

the heat is burning my feet,

and now the terror

comes

facing up.

I'm all in pain and the mellow tarmac

makes my heavy walking

desire.

The wilderness around pulls me toward it,

on the road that rhymes with perfect,

and there isn't

a more pleasant feeling

than when I see myself all torn,

almost at the end of the road.

I feel this in me and my will

approves.

I'm waiting for something to happen

out of nothing,

a final obstacle comes out,

which I have anticipated

and can't get around it,

cause it stretches across the driveway,

and I can't accept now

to go off track.

An immense tree is blocking my path.

I'm being called by the horizon

which I cannot see anymore.

My will says I can

get there,

but my condition kneels me down,

and I can only

stand up.

I punch the tree with my fist.

Still alive,

I feel powerful and my brain

feels no more pain,

it turns it into desire,

and thinking at failure creates in me fear,

but will tenses the muscles,

and I plunge.

I clung onto the log

with great expansion from the first jump.

Once up I release myself

to the other side and amazed,

I find myself among others like me,

inside an intersection of thousands of roads

from which I can choose

once again,

life.

the love we free

I sigh thinking at yesterday

but regret nothing,

from dream I crave for tomorrow but

I can't tell you that I love you,

I tell you that I miss you.

I stare into the light with an eye wide shut

to look for a resemblance,

I see you looking straight at me,

and when I see your eyes wide open,

you remind me that I love you.

You always bring another day with you,

and ostentatiously take away a dream when leaving,

and want to come back only when I love you more

than our first day

of yesterday.

You wear your light all around me

and only wish that you could fly,

but know that I'm the only one

that could launch you in the sky,

without you being able to understand

that you can,

because I love you.

Once upon a time we were a *you* and *I*,

but what made you transform into *iu*

was the coincidence that

turned me into *bire*,

and our whole flame into *iubire*.

I mentally stray on the streets

forced to avoid heavy traffic,

and I see

that you're not in a hurry at all,

when you feel that I love you.

When you stop you have a clue,

and I go forward although

I crack,

when I decide not to lie anymore,

that I crave you and you love me.

Light toward light we see each other

amazingly attracted by the colour,

I wonder if we would've ever found each other,

without having when I love you

both reasons to blink.

With sense I am shy

and refuse to find you,

I think,

that is best for you to refuse and I to be blamed,

because we love each other perfect.

I light up a cigarette asked from the smokers,

I throw the alcohol from the glass

into my soul,

I cough and turn into vice,

from passion,

I love you.

Friday 7 pm

I'm waiting for days

more,

I despair to bring you

on the brink of despair

to hate,

my love,

your past with someone else,

to wish for me to kiss you

on your warm cheek.

More hours than days

have made me see no more,

only to get tired waiting.

I'm evaluating moments,

and I only manage

to separate you

from myself.

I talk alone

when others provoke me,

the sleeve shows me

the hour that passes,

it concerns me,

and my purpose becomes/is

to meet you.

At the established hour I think,

the purpose doesn't matter,

for which I blame you.

A relevant day

for which I blame myself,

but which from instinct

makes me dream

and to feel you.

Alive decisions stir me,

if what I did is good,

not in essence but in fact,

and even

help my reflex,

so I can amaze you

when you think you can

overestimate.

I chose,

you decided,

your trust made me

realise

that everything is perfect,

is shallow to me,

a night in which I drive and you,

following an unknown path,

believe that I

will be there.

Both arrived in front of me,

yours

is pleasantly stunned by the warmth.

It's cold outside and under the light I kiss you

on the warm and soft cheek,

unused with me but which

I will neglect from very close,

Friday,

after dinner.

not for me thanks

A certain time spreads,

over us, over clouds.

What should I do to feel no more?

The past is bringing me down.

If there's anything more consistent

that awaits for me somewhere,

I think that there is not much space left,

on the firmament.

Heroic I stand and get down,

I do both with ease.

Although I don't like to admit it,

when I stand I don't enjoy going downward.

I rarely make mistakes with will,

mistake is not a lie,

I gather myself from all I've learnt,

and don't recall anyone who ever doubted me.

I offer what I feel with no regret,

I adopt any distance,

I expect nothing without a bargain,

I can't believe no one is paying attention.

I've seen the truth more than once

and live a mad feedback,

I've never been under life,

I only strayed once.

From underneath I see someone over the clouds,

listening as I watch restless

the terrible and fearless immense,

and I think at what unites us both.

From everywhere I'm offered everything,

to fight I have no reason,

but on the longterm I hide,

curious to see

where my place

is,

will be.

straight fields

Why do we go and come back

too soon,

during times of wind and rains,

and what we crush inside our fist

is only garbage?

The asphalt is a tango out of rhythm,

dull,

truth creator climate,

we climb on the same branch

naked.

From green we feel a cruel desire

for blue,

we often take cover at dusk

without realising that it surrounds us

whole.

We entirely belong to an ego,

but sad

we act in alter

and

we kneel on the sunset earth

with us.

When the abrasive dust catches us up,

in our teeth

we feel the nature rotting,

because of needs which are of

them.

We kick the strength with guts,

and calm

we develop as capable goofs,

to transform the same

today also.

The children caress the living offsprings,

they fall

majestically when time is young,

and they willingly pronounce only

we want!

Broadly destinies are to be found

warm,

the rustling has force

and the eye sees only

constant.

Light flows toward the hungry

straight,

and doesn't skip the corner as we dodge,

when everything gets covered.

We motionless look toward the horizon

curious,

and ask ourselves why does it hurt,

why are the sunset facing fields so empty,

are straight?!

cordless high jump

Earth breaks us apart but from stones is rushing
water,

alive.

Smooth motion of ours under the sunset when we
fight,

with new waves of praying at suns

we dream at

uniting with the heart,

but we vanish.

Our shivering looks amaze us

quiet,

it carries us to love resemblance

when everything strikes us with insolence.

We're living a distance much bigger

than fear.

If we had a ladder to the light

sad,

We would realise it's an honour to dream of innocence.

Without giving too much effort

we love each other,

understanding that it needs

no effort.

If a single sound is touching us

confused,

scared, we don't follow a trace of truth,

but think of what we could get

from nothing,

thinking at how smooth

our flight should be.

Even the gods can find themselves in a forgotten
kiss,

selfishly,

are throwing us crumbs of pleasure,

and we pick them like goods we found,

and shock them

when we turn what we have found

in rays of pleasure.

Touches are stealing from us only moments,

warm

all fears vanish,

we won't be there to admit

that we crave

the gods' honey from a bitter

kiss.

A clear drop of cold

water

could quench our terrible thirst

only if it would spill between firm

breasts,

during warm summer nights in the soft

sea breeze.

Distances are bringing us much closer,

heroes,

from coincidence we watch each other willing,

and time burns us through warm colours,

while thinking with passion about

what would love be,

without us.

sand between the fingers

A perverse world and a deceiving land

help us live by giving us reasons to blink,

to touch our passion the last second,

and every step we make

is our first.

We distinguish silhouettes although it's nothing there,

between sunset and sunrise but a dream,

we instinctively move from down to up,

on a cross of clues which is everywhere between

light and darkness.

Nothing is fake from what we have,

helplessness is false nothingness

that often drags us through mud,

today, tomorrow, and anytime we struggle

between needs and ego.

We speak of home at past tense,

but there we bring the torch again,

which burns for all that we were and have become,

then suddenly we realise

that no one can see us.

We risk more with every hour

and win what we're left or all,

but what we are left makes us look toward all

we're left to win

from nil.

Persistence helps us get away,

destiny loves us when we love,

toward the sky we recall ourselves in time

when decline makes us look up,

makes us just be.

nature's erotica

Am I now too calm

when I have the honour to have you,

to totally undress you,

carnal,

to want you in complete nakedness,

when the softness of your skin

seduces me,

when I loose myself?

During permanent moments you attract me

to undress you,

and like a replay

you unload me

of the clothes that constrain

the strength,

you use to look at me erotic,

you make me feel insane.

You allow me to touch you,

and you're not afraid that

I hold myself cause you are fragile,

wearing only warm salty air,

as a sea I embrace you when you run,

I light you up.

I'm naked and you dress me

when our game becomes a clue,

and tantric we play along

complete,

we measure each other

and wait to

burn.

Crossed are the fingers,

our hands like to touch,

you voluptuously fondle,

trustful

you force me to be,

and I believe you when you want

more.

The thorax draws your skin,

incredible wavy pleasure,

when I surround you

you trust me and loose yourself

in showers of brutal

ecstasy,

you make me keep you close.

Hours from Eden are wearing our ex frustration,

and dress only shapes

which are alive,

sensual we feed,

and your taste of burning skin

becomes the drug I crave,

I feed.

I think we could've woken up today

embraced under the sunrise in bed,

in paradise,

without the living windows that replace the walls.

While everything drops in speed,

only the star takes your body into semi-darkness,

which I kiss.

We look into ourselves, we're getting ready,

outside everything is restless,

wishful,

we bite our lips when the sea's waves are
screaming,

the breeze coming in chills you down and I feel

when your body floods with pleasure,

wait!

I'm with you in every feeling

trying to control the whole energy,

you open

when I kiss your breasts but I've lost you,

because all I do makes you almost faint,

and also from reflex we stop,

and explode.

subconscious angel

I wake up crisp and easy,

but hardly get up in the shadow of shy light

that's coming in

through too small squares for me to catch

my strength to fly.

I move heavily toward the wall to go out,

and wanting with sick and unbalanced elan

to get power from the light, infinite vice,

I bang my head hard against the white wall which
surrounds me in perfect angle,

and suddenly feel the need to scream.

From reflex and tensed by the concussion,

I can't understand why the wall stops me now to get my power,

from where I came,

from unfulfilled vice.

why woman

You step on grass and leave flowers behind,

which are touching you tenderly,

flowers that lean to bouquet,

and you see and feel yourself.

You smell the same when you come and leave,

under your feet everything changes,

you see other women leaving particles behind,

you want them,

to smell them,

but you hate them.

Royal breed of a being constant in perfect and in
flaw,

you expect to devour,

to feed with innocence,

but finally you are the one devoured in equal limits,

unequally restrained by your own wishes,

brought to a constant by exploited vice,

by you,

a woman,

or not.

love follicle

Anytime from time to time,

coming like a bird,

like a dream,

like a cloud strained by a grain of rain,

overflows and floods you in curve lines,

it grabs you by the centre and drops you,

it throws you,

it hits you and it doesn't care,

because you love.

As now, from time to time,

anytime,

it easily feels inside of her,

inside of him like a dream,

like a bird in paradise,

it takes you flying,

it takes you down,

it gathers you,

from the centre it expands and presses you,

it collects you,

protects then leaves you,

because you love.

Then as now and earlier,

passing next to you it got detached,

like a petal,

like a chain link it attaches to the light,

weighting at minus infinite,

it burns and spreads you like a ray,

it surprises you,

invites and leaves you,

to love.

music after 00:00

Louder and louder

comes out the music from the speakers,

against all that see light

inside dark and every movement

at first blinked.

Then struck with plasma-like impact,

it pushes us with limitless attraction.

Distance has no more meaning,

from the coils the rhythm shakes us,

time flows into the past,

agitated we touch and love,

we gather under the matte sky,

we communicate

subliminal.

Nothing from the outside matters

when the abrupt light slows down the clock,

our natural mechanic is null,

only our energies' stellar flexions matter

when the morning isn't coming,

because we want this.

Light into light is absurd,

darkness is just a shield

pervaded and widened by intensity.

We dance till exhaustion,

psychologically controlled by frequencies,

bodily by the psychic,

elements' break lift us,

the end is near but we delude it,

we love each other till depletion.

In music,

in two,

into infinity.

girl who brings sex

I wash my face with both hands,

although

I've just come out of the shower,

my towel is on the hanger,

the door is open,

the vapours slip outside,

water flows out of the wall,

outside is sad and I only want to know if you,

the one from the steam painted mirror,

were honest when you said

I want only you.

To go back to repeat what I told her,

to believe what I did,

to tell her the truth she'd think I'm a mad man,

since she wants me to tell her more,

come,

go,

tear down my wall you've crashed into at the beginning,

when I conquered you,

I've hidden,

you defended,

you placed a spell on me,

you fell in the trap easier than a bird,

you came and you served me,

without knowing about the existence of the one who soothed you,

...

who brought you into dilemma,

into sleep,

not being able to foretell the power you give him.

When you smile you stretch,

when you smell you touch yourself,

when you cum you light up.

pseudolover

Let me know your name
so I can cause you pain.
The soul inside my beast
is craving for a feast,
the beast inside my soul
is taking on its toll,
your look inside my heart
is dealing with no part.

I want to know your name
so I can cause you pain.
I wish to know your name
to break away you game,
I want to know your name,
I want to learn your game,
I want to hear your riffs
so I can crush your dreams,
I want to hear your smile,
I want to hear you breathe.

Your beauty's all I crave,
don't hate me because
I'm so,
give me the best of you,
don't stop,
offer me your inner best possession,
and I,
will give you my entire
fractioned passion.

Deal with me,
caress my ego,
absorb divine,
like you would a glass of wine,
your man,
the one that gives you
pain.

I don't believe we've met
but here I am,
for you in unshaped form
but able to deform your
form,
your perfect shape of
disguised insecurity.

if my life

If my pure mind is to be written on paper
you would all feel dull,
you would all be null,
but my pure mind can't be put on paper
because my mind isn't real life.

If my life was to be written on paper
you would all fall,
and I would rise
but my life isn't on paper
because my true life is in real life.

I'm game

One of my favourite games of all
begins with the end,
when I get close to smell your lips,
then mine slip over yours
and your surprise is clear,
you
want more.

Your big eyes got me thinking:
you're breathtaking!

I play you like a violin,
your reaction makes me feel
like living everything
in one minute,
and your tunes,
your moans
take me
to passed romantic times
I didn't live,
or did I?!

A light is coming in
in horizontal lines on the wall,
it's not dark
when you mark
a verse without words,
calling me towards you
because I was gone for too long,
exploring your
other moan...

My God, you're breathtaking!

love in you

Come in,
take my breath away,
I felt you from any possible distance
but more powerful when approaching.
Close the door,
I wish we could leave it open
for the world to see
how we make love,
in
four
three
two
one body
we melt and join each other's lives,
to walk
into paradise for good
and back for more.

meet me half way

You say nothing will happen,
I say nothing bad
will occur
while doing
what you said it won't happen,
because you lie when you're honest
and beautiful when you harvest
my desire for
the.

Meet me with good wine
when I return from the future,
give it to me to drink only one sip,
it'll be enough,
I don't need more,
leave the rest in peace but don't forget
to let one drop fall on you,
so I could find my way back
to your skin.

woman on the street

So what if
I find you walking
on streets of outer space,
my space,
while you are
willing
to be alone,
but don't know
that you walk alone
to meet me?
And not to lose a day,
how would I know you want peace?

I didn't know you before
I decided to break you with a smile
on my face,
in your eyes,
you wouldn't have looked back
if you were entranced
by a desire to be alone,
but not knowing that you wanted to be
with me,
you looked
and said yes
to me,
to life.

black moon

Once upon a magic night,
with analog piano sound
bent with passion
in an electronic club at the edge of normal,
reminds us of the passion
when we were searching for each other,
hungry for us.

I drive,
you dive in the fresh hot air
coming from outside,
it's night and blue
now
when I look at you,
both,
in your dream.

Little freedom can't hurt
when we decide to roam the
earth,
to find a place to be as free
as our desires,
close to the sea
like a Big Bang boom,
we will always have
the hidden moon.

you, me, and money

Imagine if we could've had
our kiss at breakfast,
lunch,
dinner and any other moment in between,
without the need for rest or sleep,
but only for the things that matter.

If we could've had each other,
from north to south,
would we automatically have
the west to east
for ourselves to
enjoy,
without the need to conquer?

why break?

Up

is my soul when I fall
on the ground and shatter
into thousands of hot but hard pieces,
which are melting slowly
in an ocean of ice.

I hardly crawl toward my centre
from many directions,
to form once again
myself
with more passion.

Only one drop is going
the opposite way,
it follows you
carrying my awareness,
and pulling me
back
towards you.

Unnatural behaviour
opposing natural physics,
when I'm being dismantled
by a tiny piece of me
of small importance,
which I can discard,
but
only in you.

I'm being buttered in thin air
turning into fade limits,
like a comet's tail
my soul is flowing to you
driven by a drop of my eternal youth,
which
is you.

Why go
different ways
when my drop is in you?
Why break up,
when my love
is
with you?

fire in Eden

Have you ever seen a man,
a woman,
stranded in a kingdom of
theirs,
with no commitments and fears
but
children in their eyes?

Their eyes are like shiny olives,
they chase each other and they both want.
No is an impossible word
because they are only two,
and no one else is there
to interfere
with what they do.

we come from Paris

Many times
when you're alone
you feel sad
cause you're in love,
but,
you're not sad cause you're alone,
you are sad because you love.

At some point in our lives,
we all deserve this kind of journey,
a return voyage
to a place
of deep existential abyss,
a trip to Paris.

Our feel is radius
with her,
with him, or them
or us,
in Paris.

into mine

Horizon,
you are the shapeless entity
in which I fall
alone.
You do not exist for me,
you're just a blur I take for a mark,
to see if I made any progress.

son of a God

How many times do I have to tell you,
that I have nothing to say to you
when I raise from *Infierno* like a Spanish bull
and take you to the deep abyss of blue,
from where I can show you what we could've had,
when you said no.

How can I speak my silence when I fall from years
of light,
like a virgin thunder in front of you crushing the
earth?
You don't even blink because I wouldn't hurt you,
you know this even if your tears take all the dust,
around us everyone is scared by the destruction,
by my ability to hurt you with my love.

You should take cover when I tumble
towards you like a flux of all the oceans,
don't give me a chance to crush the sands to
concrete,
cause I can't see if it's a tear on you or part of me.
You didn't believe that I could be so powerful,
so scary.
I can't believe that you are calm
when I'm this fiery.

Don't rush to think I am becoming mild
when in my way around I catch my breath into your
hair,
I'm yet in power when stealing your embrace
in vain,
when I foresee a memory that comes from pain.
You're pulverised by a tornado, but still untouched,
still fresh.
I can't believe that you said *no*,
during times when I said *yes*.

Be scared and don't get close when I am trying to
hurt you,
don't place your fingers in the flames to touch
my heart.
The way I flow is scorching the entire universe
but you are still beautiful,
even when I crush your dreams.

two French girls per day

I had many encounters in my life
but none as the one when I bought my Givenchy,
and I heard
de Paris.
I say what, I say where, cause it sounds so
la guerre,
I look up I look down but behind me,
they are there,
derriere,
two French girls that search peace
with a kiss on my kiss,
in fact glimpses over our faces.

I crave what they can give
because I've seen what they wear,
I don't mind they are naked
but I care when they're shy
and play games with their eyes.
I don't like
les croutons
till they're all
dans le soupe
but the pace is too slow when I stretch
to surround both together,
in my fail to be French
I'm a man,
like good wine.

I can

I can write the best poetry about and for one
woman,
the woman from my dreams,
premonitions I didn't make but came to me from
another universe.
When saying that I am not alone,
but that I have to fight,
not other men, but all my other possible faces
that could betray me,
and lose the grip of love.

unfinished poetry

Have you ever placed your hand on the ground
when even the rocks are silent,
the earth,
like
the light is waiting for us without interference
to find each other when we're least expecting it,
to love?

a river flows uphill

A river flows downhill faster than time,
reflecting only once a certain thing at one time,
and never again rejoins that moment in its life,
its everlasting changing life that goes downstream.

A river flows and shapes the beauty,
a plane is tumbling between the rocks.
Where did you take your magical reflection,
you untamed rose that grows to child?

Down into the valley with every opportunity you
hide,
the waterfalls don't fall, they rise,
they cover all of you to make a point,
a bridge that lets only your lips feel free.

Oh, you that comes from Paradise to play dice,
to pull towards you all the chances,
slow motion of every right decision,
be ray of sun and bend to live the passion.

A river flows uphill with all your dreams
and nothing holds a grip of what it means,
a year has past in every moment and it's dry,
except for your desires waterfall to go real high.

what happened?

It used to be so beautiful,
my blood on your face is flowing away,
the images are fading in foggy traces,
from left to right in any direction,
from right to left when the heart is burning,
because I can't escape the change
that makes my head explode.

I used to love you,
I used to melt into your body.
Why do we need the end of us
if it was for us?
Everything is shapeless when I move,
I do not want to live the end of me.
I want it to happen in one of our past lives,
no more rebirth after living in Heaven.

I can't get enough of you when we're alive,
it's a sign that I'm not from this world inside.
Why do we need to be apart
if I can lose myself into your eyes?
What good is for you to go far away from me
when you say,
what happened?

rose

The piano in my head has all the keys now,
but somehow only you can play the right chords,
rose with emotion in your eyes.
Oh, the horror of the ones that can't see that you
love divine.

there

There she is,
standing.
Who would've thought that I'd be
her face of wonders.

I feel how my feet are running slow,
I feel them heavy and hard to carry,
they don't want to go where my life is empty,
there,
without you.

a state of love

On a wooden bench on the shore,
with the sea in my face and a park at my back,
up on the cliff at some hight,
I sit with the sunset sun in my eyes.

love until

Why is true love coming to you
when you're at your lowest
state of mind,
down?

As if it knows you had enough,
that you are at your lowest gravitational point,
beautiful life
in vain.

Love finds you when you're in the deepest valley,
a point of no return of sigh,
from where you can only
climb.

Love knows you're not giving up,
but just contemplating the heights
and it comes unexpected,
uninvited.

With scruffy hair and rugged beard,
skin burned by time
and your eyes squinting,
you feel.

Maybe love was going downhill too,
and it was meant for you two to meet
at the lowest point of
no return.

I guess you were supposed
to feel this way,
to be found still romantic
by true love,
destiny fulfilled.

Cali woman

Woman,
you are only hiding the truth.
I'm a European lover, expect from me
your wildest dreams.
It's hot and your hair smells like tropical butter...
I don't know where I'm heading
but I know where we are.
I'm gonna melt you with my strength,
a woman should smell good,
your odour is exquisite.
You smell divine my darling,
you're the Californian dream,
let's fly away on chillies.

meet me with good wine

Wait for me in the afternoon,
I will rise with the fall of the sun
but don't think of me,
I will be there in time,
my absence is a tease.
I don't want you to lose your belief,
but you will not recognise me anyway
due to my demure outfit.

I will be unveiled to you after I'll drink from your
wine,
and spill some on you
because this is how you drink good wine,
like sinners before pay.
I will then come over you,
and before finding out who I am
you will let me drink even the wine flowing over
your skin,
flavoured with your divine emanated essences
triggered by the feelings of me finding you.

I will pass slowly to finding your tears of happiness
which I will kiss and leave them flowing down, into
your most emotional intimacy.
I will then finally kiss your slightly open lips ending
the fatal wait,
tasting the honey of the gods activated in our fallen
in love cheeks.
We'll hear a piano song in tune with my hands on
you.
How can a reunion be so fatal,
killing and giving birth alike?

The universe is cruel for keeping us apart,
for making us feel this with no experience of us.
What should we do with this desire to reach heaven
dirty,
how can we enter a space with no limits?
Our sweat flows as a river together with the energy.
Why do we know what paradise is when we look in
us?

We must be caught in the middle of something,
punished for loving better than the gods.
Even our wine is better than theirs because it is not
infinite.
I need to have it with your bodily essence.
You shout *my god!* and I am here like I was never
gone and more,
instinctively I'm here before you even say the
words.
We're melting and it feels good,
the fire is punishing the vapours,
I am the *vanish* and you are the *pours*.

seagull of July

Go on and fly now,
fly away and far.
Take my dreams with you
to dimmed abyss of shiny blue,
where light is shy and people few.
Please, lay an egg for me
to spread the seeds of what we are,
of what we'll be,
and leave behind all that is lie,
fly away,
seagull of July.

VOW

By the power invested in me,
your light,
my soul are one,
and because we are we'll always
be
foremost forever,
for eternity.

By the power invested in me,
I choose you to be me,
both free,
as gods upon the highest mountain,
never trapped or lost,
but one,
forever in eternity.

the rapper

The city.
Ha!

I was born between two worlds of sorrow,
from one I constantly descend to climb the other.
My words are all I've got to help me stay awake,
because I believe more than I can pay respect.

Come and give me all you have, provoke me, bitch!
So I can give you what I'm not.
Words of indestructible fragility won't keep you
warm.
I'm not cold, I'm your worst song,
the song of liberation.

*I have a dream in many ways and many ways lead
to my dream,
it happens in front of my eyes while reading a
pattern,
like a beam,
like crowded highways with millions of lights and
steams.

The reason why some do succeed
is because they die in dreams.
The reason why some do succeed
is because they live with pain.

random thoughts of a man who loves the most

I would like to be able
to paint my poetry in thin air.
Now that I'm on a top floor,
in a top world,
on a rampage in control,
I'm drawing shapes from one side to another
but I need to be faster,
because my words,
my meaningless words are there,
as a diving mist
only for seconds,
only for me to see when I can't stop,
as I'm addicted
to teaching people nothing relevant,
except for something that could wake them up.

Someone puts me to this,
I'm nothing in between
because I am not the author
when my crazed random motions disturb
the air.
I'm just a reader,
not a healer.
I'm being put to this,
not meant to be the author.
I'm a traveler in outer space
with no shape like the distance,
with no start nor end,
but with the purest feelings.

Pascal is dying

Why me?
–his tormented angle of space is asking–
Why do I have to return what was given to me?
A gift is a gift!
–he says–
He speaks with the walls shrivelled by the lack of
fresh paint.
The resolution is beyond any imagination,
so fine the images are like honey, flowing with a
constant sweet density.
He leans with his forearms against the window
frame,
there is no glass,
the window is like a painting,
with no doors...
Look at my vineyard! The crop is almost ripe.
–he says–
The weather is perfectly dry, it has been like this
for over two weeks...
The best wine will be produced this year.

He stretches and picks a black grape which he
squeezes between his fingers;
the very sweet nectar flows over his dry and
cracked skin,
the seeds fall on the ground and he tastes it with
knowledge,
the membrane cracks between his dull teeth.
Yes, this is my best year...
This wine is the answer.
 –he says while kneeling backing the wall–
Not now, wind, not now my love, don't grab my
hands with yours!
I want to feel the bitterness of missing you more,
still...
He closes his eyes, then opens them sketching a
smile, and stretches his feet giving signs of a
healthy life.
Eventually, he doesn't know what will happen with
his dreamy fate.
For the first time in his life, Pascal is lying.

feeling at the end of

feeling at the end of something

feeling at the end of something

It is over the   CROSSOVER,

feeling at the end of something

It is over the   CROSSOVER,

I am cramped and feel   THE JAM,

feeling at the end of something

It is over the   CROSSOVER,

I am cramped and feel   THE JAM,

of endless end and   LACK OF

feeling at the end of something

It is over the	CROSSOVER,
I am cramped and feel	THE JAM,
of endless end and	LACK OF
	SOMETHING,

187

feeling at the end of something

It is over the   CROSSOVER,

I am cramped and feel   THE JAM,

Of endless end and   LACK OF

                   SOMETHING,

the something that had a

feeling at the end of something

It is over the   CROSSOVER,

I am cramped and feel   THE JAM,

of endless end and   LACK OF

                                          SOMETHING,

the something that had a

smaller effect on me than   ZERO.

feeling at the end of something

It is over the   CROSSOVER,

I am cramped and feel   THE JAM,

of endless end and   LACK OF

                        SOMETHING,

the something that had a

smaller effect on me than   ZERO.

I prefer the   LACK

feeling at the end of something

It is over the   CROSSOVER,

I am cramped and feel THE JAM,

of endless end and LACK OF

        SOMETHING,

the something that had a

smaller effect on me than ZERO.

I prefer the   LACK

than the perfect equilibrium

feeling at the end of something

It is over the   CROSSOVER,

I am cramped and feel   THE JAM,

of endless end and   LACK OF

                                        SOMETHING,

the something that had a

smaller effect on me than   ZERO.

I prefer the   LACK,

than the perfect equilibrium

of between   TWO SOMETHINGS

feeling at the end of something

It is over the   CROSSOVER,

I am cramped and feel   THE JAM,

of endless end and   LACK OF

                       SOMETHING,

the something that had a

smaller effect on me than   ZERO.

I prefer the   LACK,

than the perfect equilibrium

of between   TWO SOMETHINGS

but never touching   EITHER ONE.

feeling at the end of something

It is over the   CROSSOVER,

I am cramped and feel   THE JAM,

of endless end and   LACK OF

                         SOMETHING,

the something that had a

smaller effect on me than   ZERO.

I prefer the   LACK,

than the perfect equilibrium

of between   TWO SOMETHINGS

but never touching   EITHER ONE.

The crossover is meant to   BE TOUCH,

feeling at the end of something

It is over the   CROSSOVER,

I am cramped and feel   THE JAM,

of endless end and   LACK OF

                          SOMETHING,

the something that had a

smaller effect on me than   ZERO.

I prefer the   LACK,

than the perfect equilibrium

of between   TWO SOMETHINGS

but never touching   EITHER ONE.

The crossover is meant to   BE TOUCH,

not a nullified in   CROSS.

feeling at the end of something

It is over the   CROSSOVER,

I am cramped and feel   THE JAM,

of endless end and   LACK OF

                          SOMETHING,

the something that had a

smaller effect on me than   ZERO.

I prefer the   LACK,

than the perfect equilibrium

of between   TWO SOMETHINGS

but never touching   EITHER ONE.

The crossover is meant to   BE TOUCH,

not a nullified in   CROSS.

I remember the beginning

feeling at the end of something

It is over the   CROSSOVER,

I am cramped and feel   THE JAM,

of endless end and   LACK OF

                        SOMETHING,

the something that had a

smaller effect on me than   ZERO.

I prefer the   LACK,

than the perfect equilibrium

of between   TWO SOMETHINGS

but never touching   EITHER ONE.

The crossover is meant to   BE TOUCH,

not a nullified in   CROSS.

I remember the beginning

and this is what I miss the   MOST,

feeling at the end of something

It is over the   CROSSOVER,

I am cramped and feel THE JAM,

of endless end and   LACK OF

                                         SOMETHING,

the something that had a

smaller effect on me than   ZERO.

I prefer the   LACK,

than the perfect equilibrium

of between   TWO SOMETHINGS

but never touching   EITHER ONE.

The crossover is meant to   BE TOUCH,

not a nullified in   CROSS.

I remember the beginning

and this is what I miss the   MOST,

I feel stupid now that I

feeling at the end of something

It is over the   CROSSOVER,

I am cramped and feel   THE JAM,

of endless end and   LACK OF

                                      SOMETHING,

the something that had a

smaller effect on me than   ZERO.

I prefer the   LACK,

than the perfect equilibrium

of between   TWO SOMETHINGS

but never touching   EITHER ONE.

The crossover is meant to   BE TOUCH,

not a nullified in   CROSS.

I remember the beginning

and this is what I miss the   MOST,

I feel stupid now that I

know this is   IT.

feeling at the end of something

It is over the   CROSSOVER,

I am cramped and feel   THE JAM,

of endless end and   LACK OF

                      SOMETHING,

the something that had a

smaller effect on me than   ZERO.

I prefer the   LACK,

than the perfect equilibrium

of between   TWO SOMETHINGS

but never touching   EITHER ONE.

The crossover is meant to   BE TOUCH,

not a nullified in   CROSS.

I remember the beginning

and this is what I miss the   MOST,

I feel stupid now that I

know this is   IT.

Become, be gone but

feeling at the end of something

It is over the   CROSSOVER,

I am cramped and feel   THE JAM,

of endless end and   LACK OF

                        SOMETHING,

the something that had a

smaller effect on me than   ZERO.

I prefer the   LACK,

than the perfect equilibrium

of between   TWO SOMETHINGS

but never touching   EITHER ONE.

The crossover is meant to   BE TOUCH,

not a nullified in   CROSS.

I remember the beginning

and this is what I miss the   MOST,

I feel stupid now that I

know this is   IT.

Become, be gone but

happen   SOMETHING,

something

It is over the   CROSSOVER,

I am cramped and feel   THE JAM,

of endless end and   LACK OF

                                     SOMETHING,

the something that had a

smaller effect on me than   ZERO.

I prefer the   LACK,

than the perfect equilibrium

of between   TWO SOMETHINGS

but never touching   EITHER ONE.

The crossover is meant to   BE TOUCH,

not a nullified in   CROSS.

I remember the beginning

and this is what I miss the   MOST,

I feel stupid now that I

know this is   IT.

Become, be gone but

happen   SOMETHING,

don't leave me hanging

It is over the   CROSSOVER,

I am cramped and feel   THE JAM,

of endless end and   LACK OF

                          SOMETHING,

the something that had a

smaller effect on me than   ZERO.

I prefer the   LACK,

than the perfect equilibrium

of between   TWO SOMETHINGS

but never touching   EITHER ONE.

The crossover is meant to   BE TOUCH,

not a nullified in   CROSS.

I remember the beginning

and this is what I miss the   MOST,

I feel stupid now that I

know this is   IT.

Become, be gone but

happen   SOMETHING,

don't leave me hanging

on a thread of   NOTHING,

It is over the   CROSSOVER,

I am cramped and feel   THE JAM,

of endless end and   LACK OF

                          SOMETHING,

the something that had a

smaller effect on me than   ZERO.

I prefer the   LACK,

than the perfect equilibrium

of between   TWO SOMETHINGS

but never touching   EITHER ONE.

The crossover is meant to   BE TOUCH,

not a nullified in   CROSS.

I remember the beginning

and this is what I miss the   MOST,

I feel stupid now that I

know this is   IT.

Become, be gone but

happen   SOMETHING,

don't leave me hanging

on a thread of   NOTHING,

captured in between two

I am cramped and feel THE JAM,

of endless end and LACK OF

SOMETHING,

the something that had a

smaller effect on me than ZERO.

I prefer the LACK,

than the perfect equilibrium

of between TWO SOMETHINGS

but never touching EITHER ONE.

The crossover is meant to BE TOUCH,

not a nullified in CROSS.

I remember the beginning

and this is what I miss the MOST,

I feel stupid now that I

know this is IT.

Become, be gone but

happen SOMETHING,

don't leave me hanging

on a thread of NOTHING,

captured in between two

worlds which are not MINE.

of endless end and   LACK OF

                            SOMETHING,

the something that had a

smaller effect on me than   ZERO.

I prefer the   LACK,

than the perfect equilibrium

of between   TWO SOMETHINGS

but never touching   EITHER ONE.

The crossover is meant to   BE TOUCH,

not a nullified in   CROSS.

I remember the beginning

and this is what I miss the   MOST,

I feel stupid now that I

know this is   IT.

Become, be gone but

happen   SOMETHING,

don't leave me hanging

on a thread of   NOTHING,

captured in between two

worlds which are not   MINE.

Oh, God, why are you

                    SOMETHING,

the something that had a

smaller effect on me than   ZERO.

I prefer the   LACK,

than the perfect equilibrium

of between   TWO SOMETHINGS

but never touching   EITHER ONE.

The crossover is meant to   BE TOUCH,

not a nullified in   CROSS.

I remember the beginning

and this is what I miss the MOST,

I feel stupid now that I

know this is   IT.

Become, be gone but

happen   SOMETHING,

don't leave me hanging

on a thread of   NOTHING,

captured in between two

worlds which are not   MINE.

Oh, God, why are you

so not in   HERE?

the something that had a

smaller effect on me than   ZERO.

I prefer the   LACK,

than the perfect equilibrium

of between   TWO SOMETHINGS

but never touching   EITHER ONE.

The crossover is meant to   BE TOUCH,

not a nullified in   CROSS.

I remember the beginning

and this is what I miss the   MOST,

I feel stupid now that I

know this is   IT.

Become, be gone but

happen   SOMETHING,

don't leave me hanging

on a thread of   NOTHING,

captured in between two

worlds which are not   MINE.

Oh, God, why are you

so not in   HERE?

Outside or how the worlds

smaller effect on me than ZERO.

I prefer the LACK,

than the perfect equilibrium

of between TWO SOMETHINGS

but never touching EITHER ONE.

The crossover is meant to BE TOUCH,

not a nullified in CROSS.

I remember the beginning

and this is what I miss the MOST,

I feel stupid now that I

know this is IT.

Become, be gone but

happen SOMETHING,

don't leave me hanging

on a thread of NOTHING,

captured in between two

worlds which are not MINE.

Oh, God, why are you

so not in HERE?

Outside or how the worlds

should call this SPACE,

I prefer the   LACK,

than the perfect equilibrium

of between   TWO SOMETHINGS

but never touching   EITHER ONE.

The crossover is meant to   BE TOUCH,

not a nullified in   CROSS.

I remember the beginning

and this is what I miss the   MOST,

I feel stupid now that I

know this is   IT.

Become, be gone but

happen   SOMETHING,

don't leave me hanging

on a thread of   NOTHING,

captured in between two

worlds which are not   MINE.

Oh, God, why are you

so not in   HERE?

Outside or how the worlds

should call this   SPACE,

which I can't even call a purge

than the perfect equilibrium

of between   TWO SOMETHINGS

but never touching   EITHER ONE.

The crossover is meant to   BE TOUCH,

not a nullified in   CROSS.

I remember the beginning

and this is what I miss the   MOST,

I feel stupid now that I

know this is   IT.

Become, be gone but

happen   SOMETHING,

don't leave me hanging

on a thread of   NOTHING,

captured in between two

worlds which are not   MINE.

Oh, God, why are you

so not in   HERE?

Outside or how the worlds

should call this   SPACE,

which I can't even call a purge

because a purge is   SOMETHING.

of between   TWO SOMETHINGS

but never touching   EITHER ONE.

The crossover is meant to   BE TOUCH,

not a nullified in   CROSS.

I remember the beginning

and this is what I miss the   MOST,

I feel stupid now that I

know this is   IT.

Become, be gone but

happen   SOMETHING,

don't leave me hanging

on a thread of   NOTHING,

captured in between two

worlds which are not   MINE.

Oh, God, why are you

so not in   HERE?

Outside or how the worlds

should call this   SPACE,

which I can't even call a purge

because a purge is   SOMETHING.

This is nothing towards

but never touching   EITHER ONE.

The crossover is meant to   BE TOUCH,

not a nullified in   CROSS.

I remember the beginning

and this is what I miss the   MOST,

I feel stupid now that I

know this is   IT.

Become, be gone but

happen   SOMETHING,

don't leave me hanging

on a thread of   NOTHING,

captured in between two

worlds which are not   MINE.

Oh, God, why are you

so not in   HERE?

Outside or how the worlds

should call this   SPACE,

which I can't even call a purge

because a purge is   SOMETHING.

This is nothing towards

everything that leads to   NOWHERE

The crossover is meant to BE TOUCH,
not a nullified in CROSS.
I remember the beginning
and this is what I miss the MOST,
I feel stupid now that I
know this is IT.
Become, be gone but
happen SOMETHING,
don't leave me hanging
on a thread of NOTHING,
captured in between two
worlds which are not MINE.
Oh, God, why are you
so not in HERE?
Outside or how the worlds
should call this SPACE,
which I can't even call a purge
because a purge is SOMETHING.
This is nothing towards
everything that leads to NOWHERE
but never reaches SOMETHING,

not a nullified in   CROSS.

I remember the beginning

and this is what I miss the   MOST,

I feel stupid now that I

know this is   IT.

Become, be gone but

happen   SOMETHING,

don't leave me hanging

on a thread of   NOTHING,

captured in between two

worlds which are not   MINE.

Oh, God, why are you

so not in   HERE?

Outside or how the worlds

should call this   SPACE,

which I can't even call a purge

because a purge is   SOMETHING.

This is nothing towards

everything that leads to   NOWHERE

but never reaches   SOMETHING,

or   NOTHING.

I remember the beginning

and this is what I miss the   MOST,

I feel stupid now that I

know this is   IT.

Become, be gone but

happen   SOMETHING,

don't leave me hanging

on a thread of   NOTHING,

captured in between two

worlds which are not   MINE.

Oh, God, why are you

so not in   HERE?

Outside or how the worlds

should call this   SPACE,

which I can't even call a purge

because a purge is   SOMETHING.

This is nothing towards

everything that leads to   NOWHERE

but never reaches   SOMETHING,

or   NOTHING.

There are two types of knowledge in this space

and this is what I miss the   MOST,

I feel stupid now that I

know this is   IT.

Become, be gone but

happen   SOMETHING,

don't leave me hanging

on a thread of   NOTHING,

captured in between two

worlds which are not   MINE.

Oh, God, why are you

so not in   HERE?

Outside or how the worlds

should call this   SPACE,

which I can't even call a purge

because a purge is   SOMETHING.

This is nothing towards

everything that leads to   NOWHERE

but never reaches   SOMETHING,

or   NOTHING.

There are two types of knowledge in this space

the one we create and the one that is,

I feel stupid now that I

know this is   IT.

Become, be gone but

happen   SOMETHING,

don't leave me hanging

on a thread of   NOTHING,

captured in between two

worlds which are not   MINE.

Oh, God, why are you

so not in   HERE?

Outside or how the worlds

should call this   SPACE,

which I can't even call a purge

because a purge is   SOMETHING.

This is nothing towards

everything that leads to   NOWHERE

but never reaches   SOMETHING,

or   NOTHING.

There are two types of knowledge in this space

the one we create and the one that is,

the unalterable information that forms the
possibility

know this is   IT.

Become, be gone but

happen   SOMETHING,

don't leave me hanging

on a thread of   NOTHING,

captured in between two

worlds which are not   MINE.

Oh, God, why are you

so not in   HERE?

Outside or how the worlds

should call this   SPACE,

which I can't even call a purge

because a purge is   SOMETHING.

This is nothing towards

everything that leads to   NOWHERE

but never reaches   SOMETHING,

or   NOTHING.

There are two types of knowledge in this space

the one we create and the one that is,

the unalterable information that forms the possibility

for us to turn to form,

Become, be gone but

happen   SOMETHING,

don't leave me hanging

on a thread of   NOTHING,

captured in between two

worlds which are not   MINE.

Oh, God, why are you

so not in   HERE?

Outside or how the worlds

should call this   SPACE,

which I can't even call a purge

because a purge is   SOMETHING.

This is nothing towards

everything that leads to   NOWHERE

but never reaches   SOMETHING,

or   NOTHING.

There are two types of knowledge in this space

the one we create and the one that is,

the unalterable information that forms the
possibility

for us to turn to form,

shapes of endless penetration for

happen   SOMETHING,

don't leave me hanging

on a thread of   NOTHING,

captured in between two

worlds which are not   MINE.

Oh, God, why are you

so not in   HERE?

Outside or how the worlds

should call this   SPACE,

which I can't even call a purge

because a purge is   SOMETHING.

This is nothing towards

everything that leads to   NOWHERE

but never reaches   SOMETHING,

or   NOTHING.

There are two types of knowledge in this space

the one we create and the one that is,

the unalterable information that forms the
possibility

for us to turn to form,

shapes of endless penetration for

understanding

221

don't leave me hanging

on a thread of   NOTHING,

captured in between two

worlds which are not   MINE.

Oh, God, why are you

so not in   HERE?

Outside or how the worlds

should call this   SPACE,

which I can't even call a purge

because a purge is   SOMETHING.

This is nothing towards

everything that leads to   NOWHERE

but never reaches   SOMETHING,

or   NOTHING.

There are two types of knowledge in this space

the one we create and the one that is,

the unalterable information that forms the
possibility

for us to turn to form,

shapes of endless penetration for

understanding

the is,

on a thread of   NOTHING,

captured in between two

worlds which are not   MINE.

Oh, God, why are you

so not in   HERE?

Outside or how the worlds

should call this   SPACE,

which I can't even call a purge

because a purge is   SOMETHING.

This is nothing towards

everything that leads to   NOWHERE

but never reaches   SOMETHING,

or   NOTHING.

There are two types of knowledge in this space

the one we create and the one that is,

the unalterable information that forms the
possibility

for us to turn to form,

shapes of endless penetration for

understanding

the is,

the come,

captured in between two

worlds which are not   MINE.

Oh, God, why are you

so not in   HERE?

Outside or how the worlds

should call this   SPACE,

which I can't even call a purge

because a purge is   SOMETHING.

This is nothing towards

everything that leads to   NOWHERE

but never reaches   SOMETHING,

or   NOTHING.

There are two types of knowledge in this space

the one we create and the one that is,

the unalterable information that forms the possibility

for us to turn to form,

shapes of endless penetration for

understanding

the is,

the come,

the go,

worlds which are not   MINE.

Oh, God, why are you

so not in   HERE?

Outside or how the worlds

should call this   SPACE,

which I can't even call a purge

because a purge is   SOMETHING.

This is nothing towards

everything that leads to   NOWHERE

but never reaches   SOMETHING,

or   NOTHING.

There are two types of knowledge in this space

the one we create and the one that is,

the unalterable information that forms the
possibility

for us to turn to form,

shapes of endless penetration for

understanding

the is,

the come,

the go,

but not the stay.

Oh, God, why are you

so not in   HERE?

Outside or how the worlds

should call this   SPACE,

which I can't even call a purge

because a purge is   SOMETHING.

This is nothing towards

everything that leads to   NOWHERE

but never reaches   SOMETHING,

or   NOTHING.

There are two types of knowledge in this space

the one we create and the one that is,

the unalterable information that forms the
possibility

for us to turn to form,

shapes of endless penetration for

understanding

the is,

the come,

the go,

but not the stay.

We may convert to find a way,

so not in   HERE?

Outside or how the worlds

should call this   SPACE,

which I can't even call a purge

because a purge is   SOMETHING.

This is nothing towards

everything that leads to   NOWHERE

but never reaches   SOMETHING,

or   NOTHING.

There are two types of knowledge in this space

the one we create and the one that is,

the unalterable information that forms the
possibility

for us to turn to form,

shapes of endless penetration for

understanding

the is,

the come,

the go,

but not the stay.

We may convert to find a way,

as we cannot take the shape to space.

Outside or how the worlds

should call this   SPACE,

which I can't even call a purge

because a purge is   SOMETHING.

This is nothing towards

everything that leads to   NOWHERE

but never reaches   SOMETHING,

or   NOTHING.

There are two types of knowledge in this space

the one we create and the one that is,

the unalterable information that forms the
possibility

for us to turn to form,

shapes of endless penetration for

understanding

the is,

the come,

the go,

but not the stay.

We may convert to find a way,

as we cannot take the shape to space.

There are infinite ways to be a stray,

should call this   SPACE,

which I can't even call a purge

because a purge is   SOMETHING.

This is nothing towards

everything that leads to   NOWHERE

but never reaches   SOMETHING,

or   NOTHING.

There are two types of knowledge in this space

the one we create and the one that is,

the unalterable information that forms the
possibility

for us to turn to form,

shapes of endless penetration for

understanding

the is,

the come,

the go,

but not the stay.

We may convert to find a way,

as we cannot take the shape to space.

There are infinite ways to be a stray,

between the worlds that have no edge

which I can't even call a purge

because a purge is   SOMETHING.

This is nothing towards

everything that leads to   NOWHERE

but never reaches   SOMETHING,

or   NOTHING.

There are two types of knowledge in this space

the one we create and the one that is,

the unalterable information that forms the
possibility

for us to turn to form,

shapes of endless penetration for

understanding

the is,

the come,

the go,

but not the stay.

We may convert to find a way,

as we cannot take the shape to space.

There are infinite ways to be a stray,

between the worlds that have no edge

but even this, the nowhere,

because a purge is   SOMETHING.

This is nothing towards

everything that leads to   NOWHERE

but never reaches   SOMETHING,

or   NOTHING.

There are two types of knowledge in this space

the one we create and the one that is,

the unalterable information that forms the
possibility

for us to turn to form,

shapes of endless penetration for

understanding

the is,

the come,

the go,

but not the stay.

We may convert to find a way,

as we cannot take the shape to space.

There are infinite ways to be a stray,

between the worlds that have no edge

but even this, the nowhere,

is,

This is nothing towards

everything that leads to   NOWHERE

but never reaches   SOMETHING,

or   NOTHING.

There are two types of knowledge in this space

the one we create and the one that is,

the unalterable information that forms the
possibility

for us to turn to form,

shapes of endless penetration for

understanding

the is,

the come,

the go,

but not the stay.

We may convert to find a way,

as we cannot take the shape to space.

There are infinite ways to be a stray,

between the worlds that have no edge

but even this, the nowhere,

is,
more likely than our form of kiss,

everything that leads to   NOWHERE

but never reaches   SOMETHING,

or   NOTHING.

There are two types of knowledge in this space

the one we create and the one that is,

the unalterable information that forms the
possibility

for us to turn to form,

shapes of endless penetration for

understanding

the is,

the come,

the go,

but not the stay.

We may convert to find a way,

as we cannot take the shape to space.

There are infinite ways to be a stray,

between the worlds that have no edge

but even this, the nowhere,

is,

more likely than our form of kiss,

with no connection with the form

but never reaches   SOMETHING,

or   NOTHING.

There are two types of knowledge in this space

the one we create and the one that is,

the unalterable information that forms the possibility

for us to turn to form,

shapes of endless penetration for

understanding

the is,

the come,

the go,

but not the stay.

We may convert to find a way,

as we cannot take the shape to space.

There are infinite ways to be a stray,

between the worlds that have no edge

but even this, the nowhere,

is,

more likely than our form of kiss,

with no connection with the form

but with the *is*.

or   NOTHING.

There are two types of knowledge in this space

the one we create and the one that is,

the unalterable information that forms the
possibility

for us to turn to form,

shapes of endless penetration for

understanding

the is,

the come,

the go,

but not the stay.

We may convert to find a way,

as we cannot take the shape to space.

There are infinite ways to be a stray,

between the worlds that have no edge

but even this, the nowhere,

is,
more likely than our form of kiss,

with no connection with the form

but with the *is*.

I build a reason   TO GO THROUGH

There are two types of knowledge in this space

the one we create and the one that is,

the unalterable information that forms the
possibility

for us to turn to form,

shapes of endless penetration for

understanding

the is,

the come,

the go,

but not the stay.

We may convert to find a way,

as we cannot take the shape to space.

There are infinite ways to be a stray,

between the worlds that have no edge

but even this, the nowhere,

is,
more likely than our form of kiss,

with no connection with the form

but with the *is*.

| I build a reason | TO GO THROUGH |
| but everything is out | OF SHAPE, |

the one we create and the one that is,

the unalterable information that forms the
possibility

for us to turn to form,

shapes of endless penetration for

understanding

the is,

the come,

the go,

but not the stay.

We may convert to find a way,

as we cannot take the shape to space.

There are infinite ways to be a stray,

between the worlds that have no edge

but even this, the nowhere,

is,
more likely than our form of kiss,

with no connection with the form

but with the *is*.

I build a reason   TO GO THROUGH
but everything is out   OF SHAPE,
no matter where I go as a SHAPED FORM

the unalterable information that forms the possibility

for us to turn to form,

shapes of endless penetration for

understanding

the is,

the come,

the go,

but not the stay.

We may convert to find a way,

as we cannot take the shape to space.

There are infinite ways to be a stray,

between the worlds that have no edge

but even this, the nowhere,

is,
more likely than our form of kiss,

with no connection with the form

but with the *is*.

I build a reason	TO GO THROUGH
but everything is out	OF SHAPE,
no matter where I go as a	SHAPED FORM
my struggle doesn't	MATTER.

possibility

for us to turn to form,

shapes of endless penetration for

understanding

the is,

the come,

the go,

but not the stay.

We may convert to find a way,

as we cannot take the shape to space.

There are infinite ways to be a stray,

between the worlds that have no edge

but even this, the nowhere,

is,
more likely than our form of kiss,

with no connection with the form

but with the *is*.

I build a reason	TO GO THROUGH
but everything is out	OF SHAPE,
no matter where I go as a	SHAPED FORM
my struggle doesn't	MATTER.
Continuous space is here but NOT	

for us to turn to form,

shapes of endless penetration for

understanding

the is,

the come,

the go,

but not the stay.

We may convert to find a way,

as we cannot take the shape to space.

There are infinite ways to be a stray,

between the worlds that have no edge

but even this, the nowhere,

is,
more likely than our form of kiss,

with no connection with the form

but with the *is*.

I build a reason   TO GO THROUGH
but everything is out   OF SHAPE,
no matter where I go as a SHAPED FORM
my struggle doesn't   MATTER.
Continuous space is here but NOT
                          SURROUNDING

shapes of endless penetration for

understanding

the is,

the come,

the go,

but not the stay.

We may convert to find a way,

as we cannot take the shape to space.

There are infinite ways to be a stray,

between the worlds that have no edge

but even this, the nowhere,

is,
more likely than our form of kiss,

with no connection with the form

but with the *is*.

I build a reason	TO GO THROUGH
but everything is out	OF SHAPE,
no matter where I go as a	SHAPED FORM
my struggle doesn't	MATTER.
Continuous space is here but	NOT
	SURROUNDING,
it is inside of me and I'm its	LIMIT.

understanding

the is,

the come,

the go,

but not the stay.

We may convert to find a way,

as we cannot take the shape to space.

There are infinite ways to be a stray,

between the worlds that have no edge

but even this, the nowhere,

is,

more likely than our form of kiss,

with no connection with the form

but with the *is*.

I build a reason	TO GO THROUGH
but everything is out	OF SHAPE,
no matter where I go as a	SHAPED FORM
my struggle doesn't	MATTER.
Continuous space is here but	NOT
	SURROUNDING,
it is inside of me and I'm its	LIMIT.
The reaching for something is	

the is,

the come,

the go,

but not the stay.

We may convert to find a way,

as we cannot take the shape to space.

There are infinite ways to be a stray,

between the worlds that have no edge

but even this, the nowhere,

is,
more likely than our form of kiss,

with no connection with the form

but with the *is*.

I build a reason   TO GO THROUGH
but everything is out   OF SHAPE,
no matter where I go as a SHAPED FORM
my struggle doesn't   MATTER.
Continuous space is here but NOT
                                    SURROUNDING,
it is inside of me and I'm its LIMIT.
The reaching for something is
                        DRIVING TO NOTHING,

the come,

the go,

but not the stay.

We may convert to find a way,

as we cannot take the shape to space.

There are infinite ways to be a stray,

between the worlds that have no edge

but even this, the nowhere,

is,
more likely than our form of kiss,

with no connection with the form

but with the *is*.

I build a reason   TO GO THROUGH
but everything is out   OF SHAPE,
no matter where I go as a SHAPED FORM
my struggle doesn't   MATTER.
Continuous space is here but NOT
                                  SURROUNDING,
it is inside of me and I'm its LIMIT.
The reaching for something is
                                  DRIVING TO NOTHING,
what is this absolute gives me ONE FEEL,

the go,

but not the stay.

We may convert to find a way,

as we cannot take the shape to space.

There are infinite ways to be a stray,

between the worlds that have no edge

but even this, the nowhere,

is,
more likely than our form of kiss,

with no connection with the form

but with the *is*.

I build a reason   TO GO THROUGH
but everything is out   OF SHAPE,
no matter where I go as a SHAPED FORM
my struggle doesn't   MATTER.
Continuous space is here but NOT
                              SURROUNDING,
it is inside of me and I'm its LIMIT.
The reaching for something is
                    DRIVING TO NOTHING,
what is this absolute gives me ONE FEEL,
the feel of in-between.

but not the stay.

We may convert to find a way,

as we cannot take the shape to space.

There are infinite ways to be a stray,

between the worlds that have no edge

but even this, the nowhere,

is,

more likely than our form of kiss,

with no connection with the form

but with the *is*.

I build a reason   TO GO THROUGH
but everything is out   OF SHAPE,
no matter where I go as a SHAPED FORM
my struggle doesn't   MATTER.
Continuous space is here but NOT
                           SURROUNDING,
it is inside of me and I'm its LIMIT.
The reaching for something is
                           DRIVING TO NOTHING,
what is this absolute gives me ONE FEEL,
the feel of in-between.

We may convert to find a way,

as we cannot take the shape to space.

There are infinite ways to be a stray,

between the worlds that have no edge

but even this, the nowhere,

is,
more likely than our form of kiss,

with no connection with the form

but with the *is*.

I build a reason   TO GO THROUGH
but everything is out   OF SHAPE,
no matter where I go as a SHAPED FORM
my struggle doesn't   MATTER.
Continuous space is here but NOT
                                SURROUNDING,
it is inside of me and I'm its LIMIT.
The reaching for something is
                        DRIVING TO NOTHING,
what is this absolute gives me ONE FEEL,
                the feel of in-between.

as we cannot take the shape to space.

There are infinite ways to be a stray,

between the worlds that have no edge

but even this, the nowhere,

is,
more likely than our form of kiss,

with no connection with the form

but with the *is*.

I build a reason   TO GO THROUGH
but everything is out   OF SHAPE,
no matter where I go as a SHAPED FORM
my struggle doesn't   MATTER.
Continuous space is here but NOT
                             SURROUNDING,
it is inside of me and I'm its LIMIT.
The reaching for something is
                    DRIVING TO NOTHING,
what is this absolute gives me ONE FEEL,
            the feel of in-between.

There are infinite ways to be a stray,

between the worlds that have no edge

but even this, the nowhere,

is,
more likely than our form of kiss,

with no connection with the form

but with the *is*.

I build a reason   TO GO THROUGH

but everything is out   OF SHAPE,

no matter where I go as a SHAPED FORM

my struggle doesn't   MATTER.

Continuous space is here but NOT

SURROUNDING,

it is inside of me and I'm its LIMIT.

The reaching for something is

DRIVING TO NOTHING,

what is this absolute gives me ONE FEEL,

the feel of in-between.

between the worlds that have no edge

but even this, the nowhere,

is,
more likely than our form of kiss,

with no connection with the form

but with the *is*.

I build a reason   TO GO THROUGH
but everything is out   OF SHAPE,
no matter where I go as a SHAPED FORM
my struggle doesn't   MATTER.
Continuous space is here but NOT
                SURROUNDING,
it is inside of me and I'm its LIMIT.
The reaching for something is
                DRIVING TO NOTHING,
what is this absolute gives me ONE FEEL,
                the feel of in-between.

but even this, the nowhere,

is,
more likely than our form of kiss,

with no connection with the form

but with the *is*.

I build a reason   TO GO THROUGH
but everything is out   OF SHAPE,
no matter where I go as a SHAPED FORM
my struggle doesn't   MATTER.
Continuous space is here but NOT
                    SURROUNDING,
it is inside of me and I'm its LIMIT.
The reaching for something is
                    DRIVING TO NOTHING,
what is this absolute gives me ONE FEEL,
the feel of in-between.

THE END

is,
more likely than our form of kiss,

with no connection with the form

but with the *is*.

I build a reason   TO GO THROUGH
but everything is out   OF SHAPE,
no matter where I go as a SHAPED FORM
my struggle doesn't   MATTER.
Continuous space is here but NOT

                  SURROUNDING,
it is inside of me and I'm its LIMIT.
The reaching for something is

        DRIVING TO NOTHING,
what is this absolute gives me ONE FEEL,
the feel of in-between.

THE END

more likely than our form of kiss,

with no connection with the form

but with the *is*.

I build a reason   TO GO THROUGH
but everything is out   OF SHAPE,
no matter where I go as a SHAPED FORM
my struggle doesn't   MATTER.
Continuous space is here but NOT
                            SURROUNDING,
it is inside of me and I'm its LIMIT.
The reaching for something is
                  DRIVING TO NOTHING,
what is this absolute gives me ONE FEEL,
the feel of in-between.

THE END

with no connection with the form

but with the *is*.

  I build a reason   TO GO THROUGH
but everything is out   OF SHAPE,
no matter where I go as a SHAPED FORM
my struggle doesn't   MATTER.
Continuous space is here but NOT
                        SURROUNDING,
it is inside of me and I'm its LIMIT.
The reaching for something is
              DRIVING TO NOTHING,
what is this absolute gives me ONE FEEL,
       the feel of in-between.

THE END

but with the *is*.

I build a reason   TO GO THROUGH

but everything is out   OF SHAPE,

no matter where I go as a SHAPED FORM

my struggle doesn't   MATTER.

Continuous space is here but NOT

                 SURROUNDING,

it is inside of me and I'm its   LIMIT.

The reaching for something is

         DRIVING TO NOTHING,

what is this absolute gives me ONE FEEL,

the feel of in-between.

THE END

I build a reason   TO GO THROUGH

but everything is out   OF SHAPE,

no matter where I go as a SHAPED FORM

my struggle doesn't   MATTER.

Continuous space is here but NOT

                              SURROUNDING,

it is inside of me and I'm its LIMIT.

The reaching for something is

                    DRIVING TO NOTHING,

what is this absolute gives me ONE FEEL,

            the feel of in-between.

THE END

but everything is out   OF SHAPE,
no matter where I go as a SHAPED FORM
my struggle doesn't   MATTER.
Continuous space is here but NOT
                    SURROUNDING,
it is inside of me and I'm its LIMIT.
The reaching for something is
                    DRIVING TO NOTHING,
what is this absolute gives me ONE FEEL,
            the feel of in-between.

THE END

no matter where I go as a SHAPED FORM
my struggle doesn't   MATTER.
Continuous space is here but NOT
                              SURROUNDING,
it is inside of me and I'm its LIMIT.
The reaching for something is
                    DRIVING TO NOTHING,
what is this absolute gives me ONE FEEL,
          the feel of in-between.

THE END

my struggle doesn't   MATTER.
Continuous space is here but NOT
                    SURROUNDING,
it is inside of me and I'm its LIMIT.
The reaching for something is
                    DRIVING TO NOTHING,
what is this absolute gives me ONE FEEL,
            the feel of in-between.

THE END

Continuous space is here but NOT
                              SURROUNDING,
it is inside of me and I'm its LIMIT.
The reaching for something is
                    DRIVING TO NOTHING,
what is this absolute gives me ONE FEEL,
            the feel of in-between.

THE END

SURROUNDING,

it is inside of me and I'm its LIMIT.

The reaching for something is

DRIVING TO NOTHING,

what is this absolute gives me ONE FEEL,

the feel of in-between.

THE END

it is inside of me and I'm its LIMIT.
The reaching for something is
                    DRIVING TO NOTHING,
what is this absolute gives me ONE FEEL,
            the feel of in-between.

THE END

The reaching for something is

         DRIVING TO NOTHING,

what is this absolute gives me ONE FEEL,

      the feel of in-between.

THE END

DRIVING TO NOTHING,
what is this absolute gives me ONE FEEL,
the feel of in-between.

THE END

what is this absolute gives me ONE FEEL,

the feel of in-between.

THE END

the feel of in-between.

THE END

THE END

Post Ludus

Ibiza is mine

I claim this beach in the name of both of us,
she'll love it and instantly feel at home and safe.
She will provide for me way more than I can
provide for her,
but I will still do my best to provide for her,
to love her with no mercy.
Oh, holy land, island of unholy people that will still
reach Heaven,
many of whom want to watch the sunrise in
complete silence...

I claim you for myself and her, and us to come.

You are mine because we called each other.

You stopped calling when we got together.

Don't worry, I've gathered your loud calling from around the world.

No one can hear it endlessly anymore.

I heard you and I came late, but I did.

Thank you for waiting without hopelessness!

the most powerful weapon is love

How else
can you reconcile
with the woman you love,
if not
by continuously celebrating
the wonderful moments
you both shared,
for eternity,
together,
to
get
her.

Printed in Great Britain
by Amazon

86285770R00155